IMALS

WOLVES

BY
KATE
RIGGS

CREATIVE EDUCATION • CREATIVE PAPE

Published by Creative Education and
Creative Paperbacks
P.O. Box 227, Mankato, Minnesota 56002
Creative Education and Creative Paperbacks are
imprints of The Creative Company
www.thecreativecompany.us

Design by The Design Lab
Production by Angela Korte and Colin O'Dea
Art direction by Rita Marshall
Printed in the United States of America

Photographs by Alamy (Arco Images GmbH, image-
BROKER), Dreamstime (Dmitrij), Getty Images (Ian
Mcallister/National Geographic Image Collection),
iStockphoto (Steve Geer, Nathan Hobbs, iculizard,
jeanro, kjekol, Serdar Uckun, zokru), Minden Pictures
(Jim Brandenburg, Klein and Hubert, Konrad Wothe)

Library of Congress Cataloging-in-Publication Data
Names: Riggs, Kate, author.
Title: Wolves / Kate Riggs.
Series: Amazing animals.
Includes bibliographical references and index.
Summary: This revised edition surveys key aspects of
wolves, describing the wild dogs' appearance, be-
haviors, and habitats. A folk tale explains how these
creatures are different from dogs.
Identifiers: ISBN 978-1-64026-210-2 (hardcover)
/ ISBN 978-1-62832-773-1 (pbk) / ISBN 978-1-
64000-335-4 (eBook)
This title has been submitted for CIP processing under
LCCN 2019937903.

CCSS: RI.1.1, 2, 4, 5, 6, 7; RI.2.2, 5, 6, 7, 10;
RI.3.1, 5, 7, 8; RF.1.1, 3, 4; RF.2.3, 4

First Edition HC 9 8 7 6 5 4 3 2 1
First Edition PBK 9 8 7 6 5 4 3 2 1

Table of Contents

Wolves are big, wild dogs.

There are 17 kinds of gray wolves. Red wolves are another kind of wolf.

Gray wolves are the largest members of the dog family.

Red wolves have shorter fur than gray wolves. This fur is often gray or tan and reddish on the head and legs. Gray wolves have thick fur. Their coats can be gray, white, black, or brown. They have bushy tails, too.

With pointy noses and big ears, red wolves can look like large foxes.

Male gray wolves are the biggest wolves. They can weigh 90 to 175 pounds (40.8–79.8 kg). Males are about five feet (1.5 m) long. Red wolves are smaller. They weigh about 60 pounds (27.2 kg).

Gray wolves' tails are 13 to 20 inches (33–50.8 cm) long.

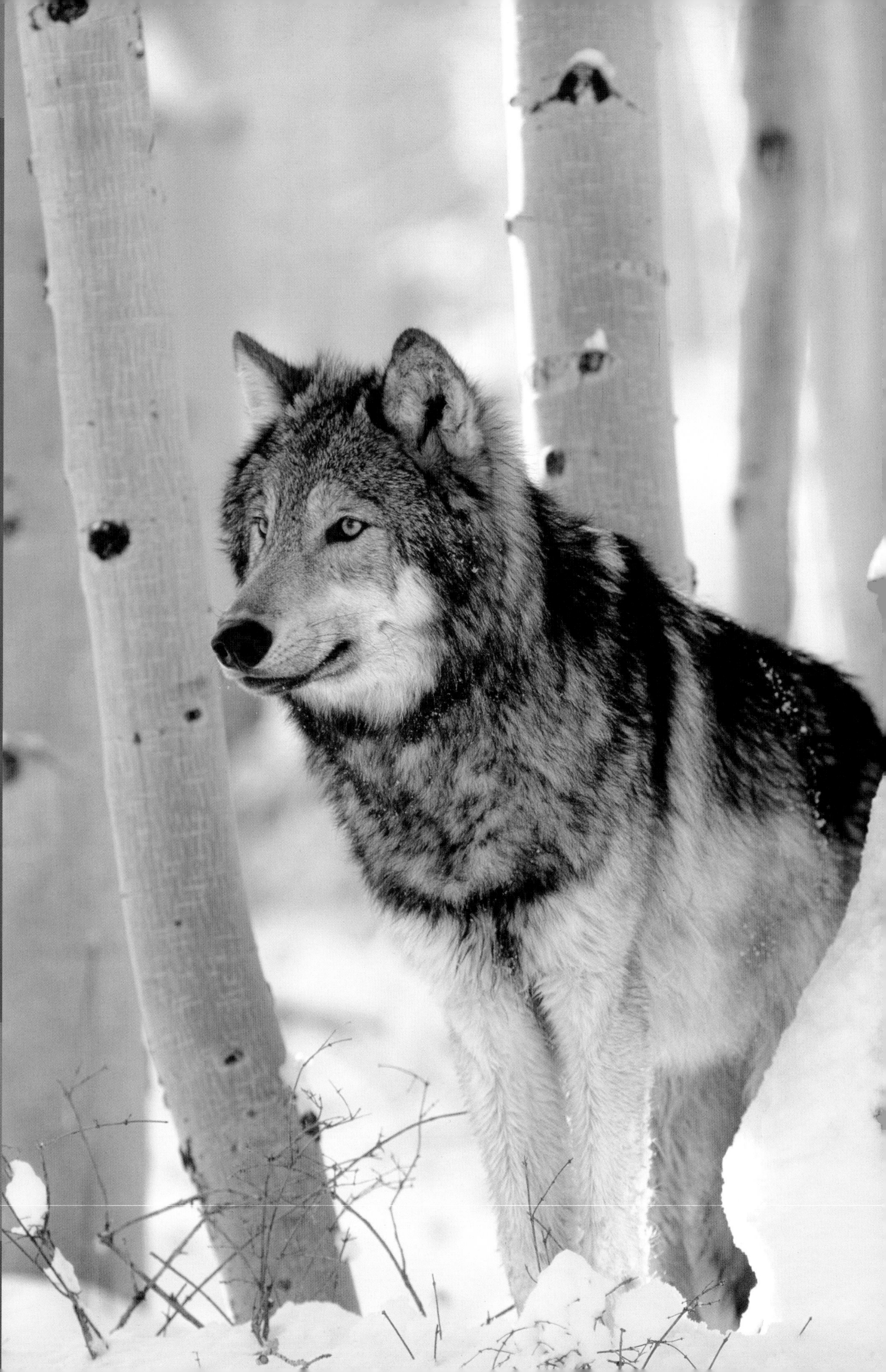

Most gray wolves live in northern parts of the world. These places get very cold in the winter. Some gray wolves live near mountains. Red wolves live only in the southeastern United States.

Thick fur keeps gray wolves warm during cold, snowy winters.

Wolves eat meat. They hunt moose, deer, and bighorn sheep. Sometimes wolves eat smaller animals like rabbits and fish, too. Wolves can go more than a week without food.

An excellent sense of smell helps wolves find food.

Wolf pups do not open their eyes until they are about two weeks old.

A mother wolf has four to eight pups at a time. At first, the pups stay in a den with their mother. They begin leaving the den to play at about one month old. They start learning how to hunt about four months later. Wild wolves usually live 10 to 12 years.

den a small, comfortable area that is hidden

pups baby wolves

Wolves live in groups called packs. Many packs have 6 to 10 wolves. One male and one female are called the alpha pair. They lead the pack. Pack members howl to communicate.

Wolves do a lot of napping, playing, and moving around.

Long legs and large feet help wolves run fast for short distances.

Wolves spend a lot of time looking for food. They hunt for up to 10 hours a day. The pack works together to chase **prey**. Wolves have to run fast to catch a deer or a moose!

prey animals that are eaten by other animals

Today, some people see wolves in the wild. Other people visit zoos to see wolves. It is exciting to watch these beautiful animals run and hear them howl!

Wolves can hear each other's howls from miles away.

A Wolf Tale

A Greek man named Aesop (*EE-sop*) told a story about how wolves and dogs are different. One day, a wolf and a dog met on a road. The dog told the wolf that he should live with people. Then the wolf would not have to hunt for food. He would have an easy life. But he would not be free. Wolves choose to be free animals instead of getting free food.

Read More

Grack, Rachel. *Wolves*. North Mankato, Minn.: Amicus, 2019.

Leaf, Christina. *Gray Wolves*. Minneapolis: Bellwether Media, 2015.

Terp, Gail. *Gray Wolves*. North Mankato, Minn.: Black Rabbit Books, 2017.

Websites

Enchanted Learning: Red Wolf
https://www.enchantedlearning.com/subjects/mammals/dog/Redwolfprintout.shtml
This site has red wolf facts and a picture to color.

Kid Zone: Wolves
https://www.kidzone.ws/animal-facts/wolves/index.htm
Check out facts, pictures, and activities about wolves.

National Geographic Kids: Gray Wolf
https://kids.nationalgeographic.com/animals/gray-wolf
Read more about gray wolves, and see pictures and videos of the animals.

Note: Every effort has been made to ensure that the websites listed above are suitable for children, that they have educational value, and that they contain no inappropriate material. However, because of the nature of the Internet, it is impossible to guarantee that these sites will remain active indefinitely or that their contents will not be altered.

Index